Who Do You Say That I Am?

A 40-Day Devotional on the
Questions of Jesus

Who Do You Say That I Am?

A 40-Day Devotional on the
Questions of Jesus

Tommy McGregor

Published by TDR Publishing, a publishing subsidiary of
TheTransMission (TransMission, INC), Montgomery, AL

ISBN: 978-0-9974817-8-5
Printed in the United States of America

Scripture quotations are from:
The Holy Bible, New International Version®.
Copyright © 1973, 1978, 1984 by International Bible
Society. Used by permission of Zondervan Publishing
House. All Rights Reserved.

For Webb

TABLE OF CONTENTS

Start Here

Jesus asked many questions when He taught. Sometimes He did this to make a point, and other times He wanted to make sure that others understood who He was and what they needed. Always, Jesus already knew the answer to His question.

This book is a 40-day look at many of Jesus' questions. Each day, you will read one of these questions and then learn more about why He said it. At the end of the few paragraphs, you will also find a question to answer and help on what to pray for. You should try to take 15 to 20 minutes a day to read this devotional, answer the question, and spend time in prayer. If you will do this, you will find that your faith will be stronger at the end of 40 days.

Blessings to you!

Day 1

Who do you say I am?

Jesus and the disciples were in an area called Caesarea Philippi. Jesus was making a name for Himself, but there were many who did not understand who Jesus was. Some said that He was a prophet, like Elijah or Jeremiah, or even John the Baptist (who were all dead, by the way). Other people thought He was a fake who wanted to turn people away from God, rather than draw people closer to God. With much confusion as to Jesus' identity, He asked the disciples the most important question: "Who do you say I am?"

These were the men that had left everything to follow Jesus. They had seen the miracles and had heard the teachings. These were also the men that Jesus would eventually call to continue the work of building the Kingdom of God. It was important that these 12 men knew exactly who Jesus was.

It was Simon who answered for the group He said, "You are the Messiah, the Son of the living God." That was the right answer, and after that moment, everything changed.

Jesus changed Simon's name to Peter and announced that it would be through Peter that the church would be built.

Before you move forward in this book, and in your life, you must stop and truthfully answer the question, "Who do you say that Jesus is?" This is important because your answer will dictate the rest of your life.

Answer the question by writing out who Jesus is to you.

Spend some time in prayer, thanking God for who He is and what He has done for you.

Day 2

Didn't you know I had to be in my Father's house?

We don't know very much about Jesus when He was a
little boy. We know about His birth, and we know, from
Luke 2:52, that He grew "in wisdom and stature, and in
favor with God and man." Then there is the story of when
He was 12 years old and separated from his parents in
Jerusalem. It was the tradition to come to the city to
celebrate the Festival of Passover. When Mary and
Joseph prepared for the journey home, they thought Jesus
was with the group of family members traveling together.
After a full day on the road, they realized Jesus was not
there and went back to Jerusalem to search for Him. After
three days, they found Jesus in the temple, teaching the
religious leaders. Everyone was amazed and surprised,
except for Jesus. When Mary asked Him why He was not
with them, Jesus replied, "Didn't you know I had to be in
my Father's house?"

Even then, Jesus had the wisdom of God's Word and a
heart to share it with others. This can be a lesson for all of
us. In 1 Timothy 4:12 it says, "Don't let anyone look
down on you because you are young, but set an example

for the believers in speech, in conduct, in love, in faith and in purity." The 12-year-old Jesus can be an encouragement to all of us that you are never too young, too old, or too-anything to learn and speak about God's truth. When the opportunity comes, the Lord will give you the words to say and the influence to be a representative of God.

When was the first time you felt like God gave you the ability and opportunity to speak wisely on God's behalf?

Pray for an opportunity to be a representative of God to other people.

Day 3

You are the salt of the earth. But if the salt loses its saltiness, how can it be made salty again?

In the days before refrigeration, salt was used to preserve food as meat was wrapped in salt to keep it from spoiling. In the same way, Christians are called to preserve this world by living a life worthy of the Gospel. In the Sermon on the Mount, Jesus called His followers to be like salt: to preserve and keep the world from spoiling. Then in verse 13, He asks, "You are the salt of the earth. But if the salt loses its saltiness, how can it be made salty again?"

What Jesus is asking is, if salt can not be used for the purpose it was created for, what use is it at all. The same can be said for you and me. If we are not living up to our potential as salt of the earth, then the world will begin to rot. As Ephesians 4:1 suggests, we should always live our life "worthy of the calling" we have received. This means we need to look at our position in the world and determine a purpose to influence the world in the name of Jesus. This is more important than making a lot of money or being popular. We are called to influence the world by preserving it in the name of Jesus. You should never lose your saltiness because you lose sight of the vision to be salt.

What can cause you to lose sight of who you are in Christ? What can help you keep your focus on Jesus?

Pray that you will live on mission for God and be the salt of the earth.

Day 4

Can all your worries add a single moment to your life?

What worries you? If you are always worried about something, you are not alone. One statistic says that almost 40% of people are constantly worried about something. Worrying is sometimes our response to not knowing what to do about something we are dealing with. The situation is important, we are not sure what to do, so we begin to worry. Even though this is a natural, common response, it is not really the best way to handle the situation.

In Matthew 6, Jesus addresses worry. In verse 25, He begins by naming some of our most basic needs and asking why we would worry about those things. He then compares us to the birds that instinctively trust God to provide for food and water. Then Jesus asks an important question: "Can all your worries add a single moment to your life?" In other words, does worrying about a situation make that situation better or worse? In my opinion, the answer is worse.

Did you know that experts say that 85% of what people worry about never happens? Jesus is telling us to trust Him instead of waisting our time and energy on pointless worrying. God will provide; He always does. Right? Don't worry about it.

What are the common things that you worry about? What will it take for you to put aside your spirit of worry and allow God to take it away?

Spend some time in prayer about your answers to the questions above. Confess your worry to God, and let Him free you of the anxiety that troubles you.

Day 5

Why do you look at the speck of sawdust in your brother's eye and pay no attention to the plank in your own eye?

Jesus was known for getting right to the issue. As someone who always looked at the heart to evaluate the character of the person, Jesus knew how this question would create an honest perspective for those He was speaking to. One misconception of Christians is that followers of Christ are instructed not to judge people. You may hear that all the time from those who claim the Bible says not to judge people. The Bible does not instruct believers not to judge but does say that you will be judged in the same way (Matthew 7:1-2). In other words, Scripture insists that we should first look at our own shortcomings before pointing out the faults of others.

For example, if someone, who struggles with lying, begins telling their friends that another person can not be trusted or believed, that individual should stop and see the hypocrisy before gossiping about someone else. Jesus intentionally notes that the plank in your eye is larger than the speck in the other's eye. If seen literally, a plank of wood is hard to miss, but a piece of sawdust could be overlooked. It is far more important to judge yourself and your own actions than it is to dwell on the flaws of other people.

What personality faults do you most commonly notice in other people? How can you keep yourself from falling into this pattern of seeing other people's struggles before your own?

Spend some time in prayer about this. Confess your struggles to God and ask Him to give you a realistic view of yourself and a perspective of compassion for other people.

Day 6

By their fruit you will recognize them. Do people pick grapes from thornbushes, or figs from thistles?

In Jesus' day, there were many false prophets. These were people who spoke falsehoods as if they were true. As Jesus said in verse 15, "They come to you in sheep's clothing, but inwardly they are ferocious wolves." Jesus was clear that these people are an enemy to the Gospel, as He said: "By their fruit you will recognize them."

The Bible talks a lot about fruit. In Scripture, fruit is the outward result of what is in someone's heart. We learn in John 15 that we will bear fruit when we stay connected to God. In Galatians 5, we see the nine characteristics of the Spirit called the fruit of the Spirit. Jesus says that these false teachers will produce dead fruit that all people will see. This question is a simple one to understand. Grapes have never grown from a thorn bush, and figs do not grow from thistles. Figs can only grow from a fig tree, and so you will know it is a fig tree by the fruit it bares.

The truth is, we have false prophets in our day, too. We must always be on the lookout for the fruit of those who are speaking. If they are producing bad fruit, we must not listen. The way we recognize false prophets is to know the difference between good and bad fruit.

What is an example of a false prophet in our day?

Pray that you will learn how to recognize false prophets so that you are not led astray.

Day 7

Why do you entertain evil thoughts in your hearts? Which is easier: to say, 'Your sins are forgiven,' or to say, 'Get up and walk'?

In Matthew 9, Jesus is getting off of a boat in Capernaum when some men bring to Jesus a paralyzed man on a mat. The Bible tells us that, because of the faith of these men, Jesus said to the paralyzed man, "Take heart, son; your sins are forgiven" (verse 2). At that moment, the religious leaders who heard these words called Jesus a blasphemer because only God could forgive sins. This is when Jesus looked at them and asked the very important question at the top of the page.

Once again, we find Jesus looking at the heart of an individual. This man was physically paralyzed; he could not walk. Possibly, he had never walked a day in his life. This was the reason that his friends brought him to Jesus. They had heard (or possibly seen for themselves) that Jesus was a healer, and they believed that He could heal this lame friend. But when Jesus looked at the man, He determined that the most important healing that this man needed was his heart. That is why He forgave the man's sins first.

Jesus' question put the leaders in a difficult position. They condemned Jesus for claiming to forgive sins (an act that they could not see or prove), but Jesus then challenged them to say that He could instead allow this man to get up and walk (an act that would have proven His authority immediately). Furthermore, Jesus also looked into the hearts of the leaders to know that they were entertaining evil thoughts. It is true that Jesus healed many people while on earth, but He came, primarily, to care for the brokenhearted and to separate the pure at heart from the evil hearted.

What are some ways in which people today can see the godly deeds of others and find fault in their actions or motives?

Pray for the hearts of others and for your own motives as you try to see the world through the eyes of Jesus.

Day 8

Do you believe that I am able to do this?

Jesus had just raised a young girl from death, and the word spread quickly that He had the power to heal. Then, two blind men came to Jesus and called out to Him for mercy and for healing. This is when Jesus asked the men, "Do you believe that I am able to do this?" After they said yes, Jesus healed them because of their faith.

Throughout the Gospels, people are healed because they have the faith that Jesus can heal them. This is important even now as we ask Jesus to heal us. It takes faith to believe that someone is God and that He has healing powers. That was true then, and it is still true now.

We are all in need of healing. Some people need physical healing, while others need Jesus to heal relationships. We are all in need of Jesus, the healer. The question is: do you really believe that He will heal you? God promises that He will heal us when we ask. In 2 Chronicles 7:14-15, we read, "If my people, who are called by my name, will humble themselves and pray and seek my face and turn from their wicked ways, then I will hear from heaven, and I will forgive their sin and will heal their land. Now my eyes will be open and my ears attentive to the prayers offered in this place." Sometimes God's healing comes in a way that we don't expect, but we must submit to Him anyway. Then He will heal us and set us on a straighter path.

How have you seen Jesus heal in the past?

What healing do you need to ask God for? Do you believe that He will answer and make your path straight? Spend some time praying about that now.

Day 9

How many loaves do you have?

As Jesus was sitting on the side of a mountain, overlooking the Sea of Galilee, a crowd began to form around Him. This happened often as the people wanted to hear what Jesus had to say. For three days, Jesus healed the sick and taught about the love of God. It was then that Jesus told the disciples to find food to feed the over four thousand people who had gathered. After collecting seven loaves of bread and a few fish, Jesus blessed the food. In verses 36-37 it says, "Then he took the seven loaves and the fish, and when he had given thanks, he broke them and gave them to the disciples, and they in turn to the people. They all ate and were satisfied. Afterward, the disciples picked up seven basketfuls of broken pieces that were left over."

There are many important lessons to learn about the power of Jesus from this story, but the thing that has always captured me is His question: "How many loaves do you have?" The answer to the question is seven, but the question was much bigger than that simple answer. Jesus didn't need to know how many loaves were available, as if He couldn't feed the crowd with six or less. Jesus wanted to include His disciples in the miracle of feeding the people. This was a team effort. While Jesus had the power to perform the miracle, He wanted to make sure the disciples had the faith to believe that if they could find some food, Jesus would provide the rest.

Still today, God is asking us how we might participate in His work. How many people do you know that need you to invite them to church? How much money can you give to further the Kingdom? Where else can you serve? How many loaves do you have?

How has God used you in the past to further His Kingdom? How might He be looking to use you right now?

Thank God for allowing you to take part in His ministry, and ask Him to prepare you for opportunities to partner with Him to "feed" the masses.

Day 10

What good will it be for a man if he gains the whole world, yet forfeits his soul? Or what can a man give in exchange for his soul?

This question speaks to the foundation of our lives. In our culture, materialistic things rule the world. The world revolves around who has what and how much can you collect in life. Many people believe that the goal in life is to die with the most stuff, but Jesus begs to differ.

In this verse, Jesus is challenging the status quo. He is saying, "You want to gain all the valuables in this world, but what then? What have you actually gained." The truth is, being rich on earth but poor for eternity is not a great investment strategy.

It is important to notice that Jesus was not talking to a group of non-believers, or even a crowd of wealthy people. Jesus was asking this of His disciples. Just before this question, Jesus says, "Whoever wants to be my disciple must deny themselves and take up their cross and follow me" (verse 25). This is not simply an appeal to avoid materialism. Instead, this is a calling to live for something greater than yourself. Following Jesus is not easy, popular, convenient, or profitable, but it is fulfilling, purposeful, and worth it.

Look back at the last sentence above. What is difficult, unpopular, inconvenient, and unprofitable about following Jesus? What makes giving your life to Christ fulfilling, purposeful, and worth living?

Spend some time praying about your life in Christ. Ask God to reveal to you the ways you give yourself to non-Kingdom building things of the world and how you can focus more closely on Jesus.

Day 11

What do you want me to do for you?

This story at the end of Matthew 20 can easily be missed if we are not looking. Jesus is in the city of Jericho and has been teaching the masses. Crowds of people are around Him, and yet he is able to hear the faint voice of two blind men crying out for mercy. Some of the crowd try to silence these men, but they yell even louder for mercy. Jesus stops and asks them a question: "What do you want me to do for you?" Jesus is the all-knowing God of the universe. He sees these men are blind, can read their hearts' desires, and still asks them to say what they want from Jesus. After they admit to wanting sight, Jesus gives them sight because He has compassion for them.

Are you blind? You might say no because you have physical sight, but think again. Are you blind? I am! I am blind to seeing the world as God sees it. I am blind to my own faults, and I am often blind to seeing how God wants me to live my life for Him. Are you blind? The first step in asking for healing is to know what your deficits are. If these blind men thought they could see, then they would never have cried out for mercy if they did not know they needed it. They would not have known how to answer Jesus' question. Instead, they might have asked for food or good fortune, when what they truly needed was sight.

When we are crying out to God and asking Him for a blessing, it is important to know what we truly need. Often times we ask for the wrong things and then criticize God for not answering our prayers. We must all look deeply into ourselves to determine what is our answer to this question: What do we want God to do for us today?

When are you most aware of your greatest needs from God? When are you least aware of your shortcomings?

Spend some time reflecting and determine your greatest needs from God. Cry out to God for mercy and healing in those greatest areas of need.

Day 12

Have you never read in the Scriptures?

Jesus was telling a parable to the Pharisees about the Kingdom of God. The Pharisees thought that they knew everything there was to know about God. They felt like they were the most religious people in the land and that God would bless them because of their prestige. They were wrong. Jesus knew their heart and knew that they could never truly understand God without truly knowing God. He called them out for their unrighteousness with the question, "Have you never read in the Scriptures?"

We learn to know God by becoming a student of God's Word. We can see the character of God by reading how Jesus loved and cared for people. We develop our relationship with God by reading the commands and following God's Word. There is no other way to gain wisdom and follow Jesus. In Proverbs 3:5-6, it says, "Trust in the Lord with all your heart and lean not on your own understanding; in all your ways submit to him, and he will make your paths straight." The most human reaction in life is to lean on your own understanding. We think something is right because it seems right to us, but

God always knows better. We must trust God and submit to Him and His Word. This means we must spend our life reading and learning the Scriptures.

What are the most common distractions in your life that keep you from reading and learning Scripture?

Dedicate yourself to God and His Word. Commit to Him that you will learn the Scriptures so that you can connect to God in a deeper way and know His truth and His way.

Day 13

Who touched my clothes?

Jesus was on his way to help the dying daughter of a man named Jairus. He was pushing through large crowds of people in an attempt to get to where the young girl was, when suddenly he was touched by a woman in need. This is when Jesus stopped and asked, "Who touched my clothes?" When the disciples heard this question, they thought it was absurd. Hundreds of people were crowding around, and Jesus was being touched by many, but He knew that this one was different. As a matter of fact, Jesus said in another account of this same instance that power had gone out of Him after He was touched (Luke 8:46). The woman that touched him had a medical condition that caused her to bleed for 12 years. Jesus healed this woman because she had great faith.

Almost every time Jesus healed someone, He did so because of their faith, and this woman may have had more faith than most. In the days of Jesus, the Jews wore long robes with tassels on the corners. These were known as prayer tassels and were there to remind them to be obedient to God's faithfulness. In the Old Testament verse of Malachi 4:2 it says, "For you who revere my name, the sun of righteousness will rise with healing in its wings." The same Hebrew word for wings also referred to the corners of the robe where the tassels hung. This woman believed that she would be healed if she touched the "wings" of Jesus' robe. She was right, and Jesus knew immediately what had happened. She had great faith, and she was healed.

Think about this story and your own faith in Jesus. Will He heal you if you reach out? Do you have the faith to take that chance?

What is it that you believe about God's power to heal?

Spend some time in prayer about the healing power of Jesus. In what ways do you need healing? Who do you know that needs to touch Jesus' wing?

Day 14

When I broke the five loaves for the five thousand, how many basketfuls of pieces did you pick up?

Jesus spent most of His three years of ministry with the disciples. He knew that one day these 12 men would spread the Gospel all around the world, so it was important to Jesus that the disciples understood everything that He taught them. These men saw many people healed and miracles of all kinds, but they continued to doubt. In Mark 8, Jesus and the disciples were on a boat, and they realized that they did not bring any food with them. They also forgot that Jesus was the great provider and always cared for the needs of others.

Hearing the discussion, Jesus replied in verses 17-19, "Do you still not see or understand? Are your hearts hardened? Do you have eyes but fail to see, and ears but fail to hear? And don't you remember? When I broke the five loaves for the five thousand, how many basketfuls of pieces did you pick up?" "Twelve," they replied.

Sometimes we can be around Jesus and not be with Jesus. We can go to church, talk about Jesus, and pray to Him, yet still forget that He is the one that turned a few loaves of bread and fish into a meal for thousands. Jesus is still doing miracles. May you never forget that truth.

What can cause you to forget what Jesus can and will do to meet your needs?

Pray that you will always remember that the Lord is a God that provides for His people. Thank Him for all that He has done for you and all that He will do for those in your life.

Day 15

Do you see anything?

This is one of the most bizarre stories of Jesus. He was in the town of Bethsaida and was healing those in need. Then a blind man touched Jesus, and Jesus led him outside of the village. Then Jesus spit on the man's eyes and asked Him the question, "Do you see anything?" In Mark 8:24, it says that the man looked around and said, "I see people; they look like trees walking around." Then Jesus touched his eyes again, and the man's sight was restored, and he could see clearly.

I have wondered about this story many times. Did Jesus' healing not work the first time? Why did Jesus use spit rather than simply touch the eyes like He had done before? Scripture does not answer these questions, but if we use what we already know about Jesus' power to heal, we can put some of the pieces together. First, Jesus always heals people because of their faith. Rarely, if ever, does Jesus heal someone that does not confess the faith to be healed. Also, we know that Jesus' power is always strong enough to bring sight to the blind.

We must look at Matthew 11:21 to understand the people living in Bethsaida. They were not faithful people. Jesus probably took this man outside the city so that He would not cause a scene in town. Then, Jesus knew that this man needed to see partially before he could receive full sight. Sometimes that is the case for you and me as well. We need to be reminded of the potential of God's healing before we are ready to actually receive healing.

What causes you to doubt? When has God taken you by the hand to prove to you that you must have greater faith?

Pray that you will be a person of great faith. Ask God to make you strong in your faith and help you when you doubt.

Day 16

Do you see these great buildings? They will all be thrown down.

Jesus and his disciples were leaving the temple in Jerusalem when one of them began to marvel at the magnificent stone structures in the city. That is when Jesus began telling them about the end of times, when the world will end. He said, "Do you see these great buildings? They will all be thrown down."

This question reminds us that nothing in the world is permanent, except for our relationship with the Lord. This world has some incredible statues, buildings, stadiums, and monuments. These structures are ones we can be proud of and travel to visit, but we must remember that one day, none of them will be left standing. The last few chapters of the Bible clearly detail what will happen. In Revelation 18:14 it says, ""The fruit you long for has gone from you, and all things that were luxurious and splendid have passed away from you and men will no longer find them." Jesus even talked about it throughout the Gospels. In Luke 21:33, Jesus says, "Heaven and earth will pass away, but My words will not pass away."

This passage serves as a reminder of the power of God and the victory that He has already claimed over Satan in the end times. Jesus will reign on the throne as king, and everyone who believes in Jesus and gives his life over to Him will live in eternity with God. Everything else will be thrown down to destruction.

What do you know about the end of times? Write it here.

Spend some time in prayer thanking God for His power over Satan and His mercy to mankind.

Day 17

Why does this generation seek a sign?

Jesus was healing a lot of people and doing miracles. He had just done one of those miracles when the religious leaders began to ask questions about signs from Heaven. Jesus knew that they were trying to test Jesus, and He asked, "Why does this generation seek a sign?"

Throughout Scripture blind faith is always valued over forming faith after seeing a sign. It is easier to see a great miracle and then believe than to trust in your heart without seeing a sign. It was Jesus, in John 20:29 who said, "Have you believed because you have seen me? Blessed are those who have not seen and yet have believed."

You can trust everything that Jesus has ever said and done in the Bible. God has been consistent since the very first day of creation. As Hebrews 13:8 says, "Jesus Christ (is) the same yesterday, and today, and for ever." You will see God work in miraculous ways in your life and through others when you focus on His Word. Then you

will know, but blessed are you when you trust first
without having to see a sign of God's faithfulness.

How do you know that God is true and real?

Pray that God will reveal Himself to you through His
Word and that you will know the truth without doubt and
having to see proof with your own eyes.

Day 18

Suppose one of you has a hundred sheep and loses one of them. Does he not leave the ninety-nine in the open country and go after the lost sheep until he finds it?

In Luke 15, we find a set of three stories, told by Jesus, to illustrate how much God loves us. First, Jesus uses a shepherd and sheep as an example. A shepherd's job was to keep watch over the sheep. Sheep are not smart animals, and it was not uncommon for one to wander off. But if a shepherd had one hundred sheep, and then one walked away, that shepherd would need to decide if he was going to let that sheep go or risk losing others to find the one.

In this example, the shepherd represents God, and the sheep represent us. Jesus is saying that we are so important to Him that He would leave the ninety-nine other sheep to search and find the lost one. In the other examples, a woman loses a coin and a father loses a son.

In all three cases, the shepherd, woman, and father celebrate when they find that which was lost.

In the same way, Heaven will rejoice and celebrate when a lost person comes to God and is saved. If you have not given your life over to God, know that He is searching for you. He will get your attention and try to bring you home. If you have come home yourself, look around for lost sheep because the Shepherd might want you to help the one rejoin the herd.

How does it make you feel that God loves you so much that He would do whatever it takes to save you and bring you home?

Spend some time thanking God for His mercy, grace, and love.

Day 19

So if you have not been trustworthy in handling worldly wealth, who will trust you with true riches?

Jesus told a story of a rich man who had a property manager. The manager was supposed to manage the money, but he did a poor job. This question can be about personal responsibility but is mainly about dedication and commitment. In the verse just after this question, Jesus says, "No one can serve two masters. Either you will hate the one and love the other, or you will be devoted to the one and despise the other. You cannot serve both God and money."

When Jesus said this, the Pharisees heard Him and were sneering at Jesus. They loved money and yet, vowed to love God as well. In verse 15, Jesus says to them, "You are the ones who justify yourselves in the eyes of others, but God knows your hearts. What people value highly is detestable in God's sight."

Jesus does not say that money is bad or that a Christian can not be rich. Instead, Jesus is saying that if you love money more than God, you will never love God enough. Money will always be more important to you. What Jesus means by "true riches" is that a lover of money will not get the opportunity to experience the wealth of God's Kingdom on earth and maybe even for eternity.

What does it mean for someone to avoid crossing the line of loving money more than God?

Pray that God will help you to love Him more than anything of this world.

Day 20

Were not all ten cleansed? Where are the other nine?

Jesus was on his way to Jerusalem and was walking along the border between Samaria and Galilee when He went to a village. Living in the area were ten men who had leprosy. Leprosy was a horrible disease that caused sores on the skin. Because leprosy was contagious, no one went near a leper. People with leprosy usually had to live alone and call out "unclean" when they walked through the village. It was the worst medical condition of that time. The ten men with leprosy cried out to Jesus to have mercy. Jesus told the men to go and show themselves to the priest in the village. As they were going to see the priest, they realized that they were completely healed of leprosy. One of the ten men went back to the village, fell at Jesus' feet, thanked Jesus, and began to praise God.

When Jesus realized that only one of the ten came back to thank Him, he said, "Were not all ten cleansed? Where are the other nine?" He said to the man, "Rise and go; your faith has made you well."

Learning to be grateful is a very important trait for your own faith and that of others. Saying "thank you" is a way of humbling yourself and denying any pride that you might be carrying. It would have been easier and less embarrassing for this man to go with the others, without thanking Jesus, but Jesus blessed this man's courage and healed him in more ways than just his leprosy, all because of his faith.

Why is it is good to develop a heart of gratefulness in your life?

Begin by thanking God for all of the blessings in your life. Think about all the many ways He has saved and healed you. Give Him the praise He deserves.

Day 21

I have spoken to you of earthly things and you do not believe; how then will you believe if I speak of heavenly things?

One night, Jesus had a visitor named Nicodemus. Nicodemus was a Pharisee and a member of the Jewish ruling council. He was a very well-known and important person to the community, and He wanted to know more about Jesus. Nicodemus was curious about Jesus and knew that He must have been sent by God. Jesus told him that anyone who wants to live in God's Kingdom must be born again.

You have probably heard that phrase "born again" before, but when Nicodemus heard Jesus say it, it was a new concept. Nicodemus was confused how someone could be born a second time. Jesus explained that everyone is physically born once but must also be spiritually born again. Then, beginning in verse 10, Jesus says, "You are Israel's teacher; do you not understand these things? Very truly I tell you, we speak of what we know, and we testify to what we have seen, but still you people do not accept our testimony. I have spoken to you of earthly things and you do not believe; how then will you believe if I speak of heavenly things?"

The older you get and the longer you are a Christian, the more you should learn and understand about what it means to follow Jesus. A new Christian should not know as much about following Jesus as someone, of the same age, that has been a Christian since childhood; but that often happens. Jesus then goes on to explain the Gospel, which is when he says John 3:16. Hopefully, Nicodemus understood it after that night. Hopefully, you will too.

What is it about the Gospel that is hard for you to understand?

Look back at your answer to the question above and pray that God will help you understand it. Think of someone who might be able to explain it to you so that you will fully understand the story of God and your salvation.

Day 22

Will you give me a drink?

Jesus was passing through Samaria, on His way back to Galilee. Samaria was an area that many Jews avoided. The Jewish and Samaritan peoples did not always get along, yet Jesus was passing through and stopped at a well for a drink of water at noon. The disciples left Him to get food, and a Samaritan woman came to get water. Usually, the women would come in the early morning hours to get water, but this woman was not very respected in the community. She came at noon to avoid the people, but she met Jesus, and He asked her for a drink of water.

Normally, Jewish men did not talk to Samaritan women, but this was not a typical Jewish man. Jesus told her about living water that is found in a relationship with God. She was surprised that He seemed to know her and love her. She went back to the village a saved person that day, and Jesus stayed in the area for a few more days to teach and speak to the people in the village.

Jesus changes people. He knows what we have done, and He knows us better than we know ourselves. He offers us all a better life than we could ever have on our own. He offers a spring of living water so that we will never be spiritually thirsty again. This is the Gospel of Jesus. Won't you choose to drink it, too?

Read the story of Jesus and the Samaritan women in John 4. What surprises you most about her reaction to Jesus?

Spend some time in prayer for those who are not connected in a relationship with Jesus. Like this woman, they, too, need to have an encounter with God. Pray for that.

Day 23

Where shall we buy bread for these people to eat?

One thing to understand about Jesus and the questions He asked was that He already knew the answers. The questions of Jesus were not asked so He could learn an answer, but rather so that the person He was talking to would know the answer.

In this moment, Jesus has been speaking to five thousand people, and they were hungry. Much like the story of feeding the four thousand, Jesus wanted to find food for them. Knowing what He will eventually do, He asks Philip, one of the disciples, "Where shall we buy bread for these people to eat?" Then in verse 6, it says, "He asked this only to test him, for he already had in mind what he was going to do."

Jesus knows all things. He knows how to form mountains. He knows how to cure disease. He knows the struggles you are dealing with, and He knows what it will take for you to overcome your doubt and unbelief. He must have known that day that Philip was in need of a challenge. Phillip's answer was a practical one: "It would take more than half a year's wages to buy enough bread for each one to have a bite!" On the surface this was true, but God never works on the surface.

To believe in God is to believe in a power greater than yourself. You can't feed five thousand people with a few fish and bread, but God can. You can't change the world and save people from death, but God can. You can't overcome your struggles and live a full life through your own power, but in Christ you can do it. As a matter of fact, you can do all things through the strength of Jesus. (Philippians 4:13).

What is the hardest thing that God has ever asked you to do? How did He strengthen you during the challenge?

Pray for your future trials and struggles. Ask God to give you strength so that you can be ready when He calls you.

Day 24

Do you understand what I have done for you?

On the night of the Last Supper, Jesus was eating with the disciples. He was hours from being arrested and in his last full day before being crucified. After they ate, Jesus, the king of the world, got on his knees and washed the disciples' feet. Then He asked them, "Do you understand what I have done for you?"

In those days, everyone wore sandals and walked everywhere. Because of this, everyone had dirty feet. It was the custom that when someone walked into a house, the servant would take a bowl of water and wash the person's feet. The owner of the house never washed the feet of the guest; it was always the servant.

When Jesus washed the feet of the disciples, they did not know how to respond. Peter actually told Jesus not to do it at first. The purpose of this was that Jesus was modeling leadership. A leader is not someone who stands up on a stage and tells others what to do. A true leader gets down and serves people. Jesus was showing these men how to continue spreading the Gospel after Jesus was gone.

Today, we are called to wash feet, not literally, but spiritually. God calls all believers to follow His lead and become a servant leader to other people. This means we must look for ways to serve the needs of others. At the end of the foot washing, Jesus looks up and says to the disciples: "I have set you an example that you should do as I have done for you. Very truly I tell you, no servant is greater than his master, nor is a messenger greater than the one who sent him. Now that you know these things, you will be blessed if you do them" (John 13:15-17).

Make a list of ways you think you can model servant leadership to others.

Thank God for the ways He has modeled leadership for you, and pray that He will allow you to put those examples of leadership into practice.

Day 25

Don't you know me, even after I have been among you such a long time?

Even though Jesus spent three years teaching and healing people, He spent most of that time with the twelve disciples. The reason for this was because they were going to be sent all over the known world to spread the Gospel. Jesus knew He had three years to teach them everything they needed to live fully for Him, even to death. They had seen Him heal the sick, raise the dead, and teach God's Word to the thousands. They spent every day with Jesus so that they would know Him. Then in John 14, Jesus told them that He is the truth, the life, and the way, and that if you know Him, you will know God.

That was when Phillip said, "Lord, show us the Father and that will be enough for us." Then Jesus said: "Don't you know me, Philip, even after I have been among you such a long time? Anyone who has seen me has seen the Father."

Sometimes we read about the disciples and think, "How could they not get it?" We think that they could have been smarter and understood more. But, we have the advantage of having the whole Bible in front of us, to read what happened before and after this conversation in John. We have Paul's writings to help us learn even more than the disciples could have learned at the time. We have a perspective of God's story that Philip and the others did not have, and yet, often times we still struggle to believe who Jesus really is.

Think about all the times you have wondered if it is true or not. Think about the times you have forgotten what Jesus said and did, and you choose to live as if you had never heard. We are forgetful people, which is why we must stay in God's Word and let it teach us over and over again.

What verses of the Bible can you use to remember who God is and how much He loves you?

Say a prayer using the verses you thought of for the question above. Memorize them and pray them often as you seek to commit to remember who Jesus is.

Day 26

What is your name?

Jesus and the disciples had sailed across the Sea of Galilee to an area called Gerasenes. When they stepped foot on land a demon-possessed man was there to confront Jesus. This man had caused a lot of problems for the people in the region. He had be chained up and sent out, but nothing could control the man. The demon that lived in the man was from Satan, and it had control of the man. The demon recognized Jesus and said, "What do you want with me, Jesus, Son of the Most High God? I beg you, don't torture me!" Jesus asked his name, and he said that his name was Legion because many demons lived in him. At once, Jesus made the demons leave the man and enter into a herd of pigs.

There are many lessons to learn about God from this story. First, the demons knew who Jesus is, and yet Jesus has the power to destroy them. I think the point that I hope you get from this situation is the love and care that Jesus took on this man. This man was a problem to the people in Gerasenes. This man was cursed by demons and could have just as easily been killed. But Jesus had compassion on the man and even asked his name. This was a chance to find out who he really was. Jesus knew that this man could be freed from the demons and live a regular life again.

I know this is a strange story and one that we struggle to understand. What is demon possession and what happened to the pigs? (read Luke 8:33) The best part of this story is how much Jesus cared for this man. You need to always remember that Jesus loves you no matter what you have done, and He wants to restore you back to Himself. If He can do it for Legion, He can do it for you and me as well.

Thinking about how much God must have loved someone like Legion, what does that say about how much He loves you?

Spend some time thanking God for the love He has for you and for others.

Day 27

Which of these three in your opinion was neighbor to the robber's victim?

The Bible tells us to love our neighbor, but who is your neighbor? Is it the person who lives next door? Is it your best friend, or could it be someone you might think of as an enemy? Jesus was asked this same question, and he told the parable of the Good Samaritan.

In the story, a Jewish man is walking on the road from Jerusalem to Jericho when he is beaten, robbed, and left to die on the road. A priest walks by and sees the man and actually moves to the other side of the road to pass by. Another religious leader passes the man and does not stop. Then a Samaritan man, considered an enemy to many Jews, comes by, sees the man, and takes him to a doctor. The Samaritan pays the doctor and even offers to come back to give more if needed. It was then that Jesus asked the listeners, "Which of these three in your opinion was the neighbor to the robber's victim?"

Obviously, the Samaritan was the neighbor because he loved the man and cared for him. This famous story is one of the most important lessons that Jesus taught.

Throughout the Bible, we learn that the most important commandment is to love God, and the second is to "Love your neighbor as yourself" (Mark 12:31). This is the cornerstone of what it means to be a follower of Jesus. It doesn't matter where your neighbor is from, what they look like, or even how poorly they may have treated you in the past. The only thing that matters is that God commands you to treat them like you would want to be treated. What if you had been the man that was beaten? Which of the three passersby would Jesus have been?

Describe how the world would be if all Christians made it a priority to be the Good Samaritan.

Pray for opportunities to love your neighbor and be the Good Samaritan.

Day 28

Do you want to be well?

Once, when Jesus was in Jerusalem for a festival, He walked by the pool called Bethesda. This was a large pool, and it was covered with hundreds of disabled people who were blind, lame, and paralyzed. The reason they were there was because they all believed a myth that an angel would stir the water and heal the first person to get in after the first ripple. Jesus looked and saw one man who had been sitting there for thirty-eight years. This man could not walk and was not able to get close enough to get in the pool to be healed. This is when Jesus asked him an interesting question: "Do you want to get well?"

You would think that the answer to this question would be obvious because the man had been trying to get well for 38 years. You might even think that Jesus would have asked him something else like, "Can I help you get into the water?" or maybe, "Can I heal you?" The truth is, Jesus always looks at the condition of the heart before the physical needs of an individual. For 38 years, this man had wasted his life on a myth that was not even true. In those years, he could have been trying to find another cure or worked to improve what strength he might have had. Instead, he became complacent and maybe even lazy. So, to ask if he really wanted to be well, was actually a good question.

The point is to think about what you really want in life and if you are working to reach that goal or just waiting on some mythical idea to magically get you there. The question for you is, "Do you really want to reach that goal?"

What goal are you waiting on to happen but possibly not putting in the work to achieve?

Spend some time praying for your goals and the process you will need to take to reach them. Ask for God's help and for Him to show you the steps to take.

Day 29

Why are you thinking these things in your hearts?

Jesus was teaching in a home that was so crowded that no one else could get in. Four friends of a paralyzed man wanted to get their friend to Jesus but could not find a way in the house. So, they climbed up on the house, made a hole in the roof, and lowered the man in. In verse 20 we read, "When Jesus saw their faith, He said, 'Friend, your sins are forgiven'."

There were some Pharisees and religious leaders in the room who began to wonder to themselves how Jesus could forgive sins. To them, this was blasphemy. Then, beginning in verse 22, it says, "Jesus knew what they were thinking and asked, 'Why are you thinking these things in your hearts? Which is easier: to say, Your sins are forgiven, or to say, Get up and walk? But I want you to know that the Son of Man has authority on earth to forgive sins.' So he said to the paralyzed man, 'I tell you, get up, take your mat and go home.' Immediately he stood up in front of them, took what he had been lying on and went home praising God."

There are so many lessons that we can take away from this story. First, how about those four friends who did whatever needed to be done to get their friend in front of Jesus? Second, how awesome would it have been to see a paralyzed man get healed and get up and walk? Or, maybe you are wondering, how do you make a hole in someone's roof without the whole house caving in? All of these are good points, but the question today relates to the fact that Jesus read the minds of these religious men and knew what they were thinking. He knew their hearts and called them out. May we all have the heart of the four friends, loving and compassionate, and not that of the Pharisees who did not know God.

What heart characteristics do you hope that God sees in your heart?

Pray that God will give you the heart of those friends and allow you to love your friends enough to bring them to the feet of Jesus.

Day 30

Why are you trying to trap me?

The Pharisees made it their mission to catch Jesus in a false teaching so that they could have him arrested or killed. Throughout the Gospels, you can find numerous examples of this. On this day, the Pharisees asked Jesus a question about paying taxes. The question was phrased so that if Jesus said that they should not pay taxes, which were unfair, the Romans would probably arrest Jesus. But if Jesus said to pay the taxes, many of the people might think Jesus was working with the government, and they might not follow Him. Jesus knew it was a trick, which is why He asked why they were trying to trap Him.

To answer the question, Jesus asked for a coin, and then He asked whose face was on the coin. The answer was Caesar. In verse 17, Jesus said, "Give back to Caesar what is Caesar's and to God what is God's."

This was Jesus' perspective about the world. The world has laws and rules, and God has laws and rules. Paying taxes was a governmental law, and it did not conflict with doing God's law. Jesus was saying that we should always remember that ultimately, God rules over Caesar, but we should follow both sets of laws and rules. In fact, Jesus is saying that you are following God's rule by obeying Caesar's law of paying taxes. That is what it means to be a citizen of the Kingdom of God while living in the world.

What are some other examples today of how we should "Give back to Caesar what is Caesar's and to God what is God's?"

Pray that our government will always be fair and open to believers to worship and follow God's teaching and law, as well as its own.

Day 31

Can any of you prove me guilty of sin? If I am telling the truth, why don't you believe me?

Jesus was having a heated discussion with the religious leaders about who He was in relation to them. They all claimed to be the children of Abraham, but if they truly saw Abraham as their father, they would do as Abraham did. As Jesus said in verse 40, "As it is, you are looking for a way to kill me, a man who has told you the truth that I heard from God. Abraham did not do such things." The question from Jesus for today is, "Can any of you prove me guilty of sin?" Jesus was sinless which allowed Him to become the perfect sacrifice on the cross for our sins.

Everything Jesus ever said was true. This entire discussion began because Jesus said in John 8:31-32, "If you hold to my teaching, you are really my disciples. Then you will know the truth, and the truth will set you free." Then, Jesus asked and answered his own question in verse 43, "Why is my language not clear to you? Because you are unable to hear what I say?" and then in verse 47, He ends with, "Whoever belongs to God hears

70

what God says. The reason you do not hear is that you do not belong to God."

When someone does not know the truth, they will not understand the truth when they hear it. There are many opportunities to hear false statements presented as truth. Our culture tries to teach us things that are not true, and it is up to us to learn the difference. The way to decide truth over non-truth is to use Scripture as a guide. God's Word is always truthful, and anything that contradicts Scripture is not worth listening to.

What is a non-truth that you have heard from worldly voices that does not line up with God's truth?

Pray that you will learn the difference between truth and non-truth. Ask God to show you His truth in the Word.

Day 32

Can you drink the cup I am going to drink?

What does it take to follow Jesus? The word "follow" gives us a clue. To follow someone means that we stay behind them and go where they go. The game Follow the Leader is a great example of this. In Follow the Leader, the leader does many gestures and walks in different directions, while the followers attempt to keep up. They must do exactly as the leader does. Living in a relationship with Jesus is like a life-long game of Follow the Leader.

Jesus was clear that following Him would not be easy. In Matthew 16:24, Jesus said, "If anyone would come after me, let him deny himself and take up his cross and follow me." To deny yourself and take up your cross means to follow Jesus to death. This will probably not mean physical death, but it certainly will be death of many pleasurable things in this world. In this passage of Matthew 20, the mother of James and John boldly asks Jesus if her two sons can sit on either side of Jesus in the throne room of Heaven. (Yes, she actually asked Jesus that!) Jesus' response to the two young men was, "Can you drink the cup I am going to drink?" In other words, He is asking if they are willing to follow Him to death. This is a question that Jesus is asking each of us.

Following Jesus takes sacrifice. If you are not sacrificing desires, opportunities, relationships, etc. to follow Jesus, you might not be following Him closely enough. In order to follow this Leader, you must be willing to follow Him anywhere. You must be willing to blindly drink of the cup He leads you to drink.

What have you given up to follow Jesus? What is God asking you to give up now to follow Him?

Spend some time praying over the things listed above. How will you follow your Leader closer and become more dedicated to living for Christ?

Day 33

Are you asleep? Could you not keep watch for one hour?

Have you ever been so tired that you simply could not stay awake? Maybe you were in a classroom and kept dosing off while the teacher was teaching, or trying to watch a movie when you were too tired to focus. For Peter and the disciples, they were in the garden of Gethsemane, and Jesus was about to be arrested and put to death. Jesus had asked them to keep watch while He went to be alone and pray. When Jesus came back, the disciples were asleep, and Jesus was frustrated. In verse 38, He tells them, "watch and pray so that you will not fall into temptation. The spirit is willing, but the flesh is weak." It is one thing to fall asleep when someone has asked you to help them, but it is worse when God calls you to serve Him, and you are asleep on the job. Jesus tells them that they need to keep themselves from temptation, admitting that the flesh is weak.

Sometimes we may stay physically awake but fall asleep spiritually. God might ask us to help Him build the Kingdom, but we are too tired to do the job well. If we are not alert and ready, we might sleep right through a moment that would have given us great strength in our faith.

Eventually Peter learned this lesson and wrote in 1 Peter 5:8, "Be sober-minded; be watchful. Your adversary the devil prowls around like a roaring lion, seeking someone to devour." We must be ready when God calls us to serve Him. We must stay awake.

What are some ways in which you can stay alert in your faith and remain awake for God's call for you to stand guard?

Spend some time in confession for when you have spiritually fallen asleep on your watch. Pray that God will help you be alert in your faith as you lean on the Spirit that is willing.

Day 34

Do you think I cannot call upon my Father and he will not provide me at this moment with more than twelve legions of angels?

The night that Jesus was to be arrested and put to death, He was in the garden with some of the disciples. The soldiers came, led by Judas, to arrest Jesus, and the disciples began to fight back. Peter, doing what he believed was right, pulled out a sword and cut off one of the soldier's ears. Jesus told Peter to put the sword away because this was what was supposed to happen. Then Jesus asked this question: "Do you think I cannot call upon my Father and He will not provide me at this moment with more than twelve legions of angels?" With that, He healed the man's ear and was taken away.

A legion represented 5,000 soldiers, or in this case, angels. Angels are not described in Scripture as small, delicate creatures with white wings, but as mighty soldiers with weapons. Jesus reminds the disciples of His power to call down 60,000 warriors to defend Him within seconds, but that would not have fulfilled His mission.

In Romans 6:23 we read, "For the wages of sin is death, but the gift of God is eternal life in Christ Jesus our Lord." A wage is a payment for something. This verse tells us that the payment for sin is death, but Jesus' death brings life to us if we will believe. Jesus could have done it another way. He could have defeated Satan on that day in the garden, but that would not have allowed us to make the choice to follow God. When you choose something, you do so because you really want it, but when something is always there for you to have, you never fully appreciate it. This is why it had to be this way. That is how much God truly loves you.

How would you have saved the world from sin if you had been God? Do you really think your plan would have worked?

Spend time in prayer by thanking God for His plan of salvation.

Day 35

My God, my God, why have you forsaken me?

Jesus hung on the cross for you and me. Jesus died on that cross to save us from our sin. Sin separates us from God. God is perfect and can not look on us in sin. This is why Jesus came to die as a sacrifice for us all. As Romans 5:8 says, "But God demonstrates his own love for us in this: While we were still sinners, Christ died for us."

This is most likely the hardest question Jesus asked. This is the moment when all the sin of the world came upon Jesus, and for a brief moment, God had to look away. Jesus felt that moment and cried out to His Father, "Why have you forsaken me?"

If there was ever a moment in Scripture that put our sin and Jesus' sacrifice into perspective, it would have to be this question. It is our fault that Jesus felt forsaken. It is our sin that made God turn His face. Now, the question is, what do we do about it? We can not become sinless, but we can be conscience of our sin and pursue holiness. We can give ourselves to God because of the sacrifice He made for us. This question should not go unanswered by us as we understand our part in hanging Jesus on a cross. Let this guide you and your commitment to Jesus for the rest of your life.

How can you commit your life to God as a repayment for Jesus' death for your sin?

Give God praise for the sacrifice of His Son for your sake. Spend some time thanking God for the cross and committing to Jesus to live for Him.

Day 36

Why are you crying? Who is it you are looking for?

The morning Jesus rose from the dead, Mary Magdalene went to the tomb and discovered that it was empty. Her first reaction was to cry. Then she saw Jesus but did not recognize him and mistakenly thought he was the gardener. This is when Jesus asked her, "Why are you crying? Who is it you are looking for?" She asks where Jesus' body was taken, and Jesus calls her name, and Mary recognizes Jesus.

This must have been an amazing moment. Mary did not expect to see Jesus alive. She must have cried even more. At that moment, Jesus told her to tell the disciples that He had risen from the dead, just as He said that He would.

Does Jesus still surprise you? Are you close enough to Him that you are looking for Him and are tearfully surprised when you see Him? I hope so because Jesus can show up anywhere, through other people and opportunities that we would never have dreamed of having. In Proverbs 15:3 we see that, "The eyes of the

LORD are in every place". The question is, are you looking for Jesus. If you are, you will find Him.

How have you seen Jesus surprise you in the way that He loves you?

Spend some time in prayer and think about that day at the tomb. Thank God for His power over death and unending love for you.

Day 37

What are you discussing together as you walk along?

The day Jesus rose from the dead, two men were walking along a road to a village called Emmaus, and they were talking about all that had happened with Jesus. Then the risen Jesus walked up along side of them and asked, "What are you discussing together as you walk along?" They did not recognize Jesus, and so thinking He must be a foreigner, they told Him about the cross and the news of the resurrection. Jesus walked with them and reminded them what the Old Testament said about how the Messiah would suffer and then rise from the dead. As they reached their home, they invited Jesus in, and when he sat at the table and broke the bread, they saw that this stranger was Jesus.

This story is a picture of walking with Jesus. Many times, a relationship with God is described as a journey or a walk. When we are following Jesus, we are walking with Him and learning as we go. These men did not know they were walking with Jesus, but when you know God, you know who it is you are following.

When we walk with Jesus, we step in His footprints and learn from His teaching. We have God's Word as our map, and we have other believers to serve as mentors to teach us God's way. Ultimately, we have Jesus himself, walking in relationship with us, never leaving our side. That is what it means to walk with Jesus, discussing life, as you walk along.

When have you felt close to Jesus? What were the circumstances, and what did you learn from it?

Thank God for his Son and for the intimate relationship that He offers. Pray that you will always seek to walk with Jesus and learn to step as He steps.

Day 38

Did not the Christ have to suffer these things and then enter his glory?

While on the road to Emmaus with the two men, Jesus told the men all about what the Old Testament prophecy said of the Messiah and how He would be crucified and raised from the dead. This is when Jesus asked, "Did not the Christ have to suffer these things and then enter his glory?"

This is an important question for every person to answer for themselves because it is the cornerstone of the Gospel. We must all understand that we are dead in our sin (Romans 3:23) and in need of a Savior. Christ did not want to suffer; He had to suffer so that those who believe would have eternal life (John 3:16). Then, Jesus had to rise from the dead to overcome death in order for us to worship a living God in glory (John 11:25).

Do you believe this? Deep down in your heart, do you believe that Jesus had to die for you, and that He would have died even if you were the only one needing to be saved? This is the Gospel, and it is the message that all people need to hear.

Write below a summary of the Gospel in your own words.

Re-read your Gospel summary and pray that you will live it and share it when God opens up an opportunity to do so.

Day 39

Friends, haven't you any fish?

The last thing that Peter did before Jesus died on the cross was to deny him three times, just as Jesus had predicted. This weighed heavy on Peter, and eventually Peter went back to doing what he did before meeting Jesus. Peter went fishing. Joined by a few other disciples, the fishermen were in a boat, casting their nets. Then Jesus walked up on shore and asked them, "Friends, haven't you any fish?" They replied, "no" and Jesus told them to put the nets on the other side. When they did, they caught more fish than ever before, and then they knew that the man was Jesus. Peter could not wait to paddle back to shore, so he jumped in the water and swam back. Then Jesus made a fire, and they had breakfast there on the beach.

There is no end to what we can learn from Jesus, even professional fishermen need a fishing lesson from Jesus to catch fish. The question Jesus asked was not if there were any fish to be caught or if they wanted Him to start the fire, but if they had caught any yet. Jesus was the one who actually caught those fish, but He did so through Peter's net. This is a lesson for us to understand about how God works in us. He provides the way, but we must do our part to catch the fish that God has provided. As Paul said in Philippians 4:19, "And my God will supply every need of yours according to his riches in glory in Christ Jesus." Those fish did not jump into the boat, but they were ready to be scooped up by the nets.

How does this story help you understand how God moves in our lives?

Spend some time thinking and praying to God for all of the many ways He moves in our lives.

Day 40

Do you love me?

After Jesus and the disciples ate breakfast on the beach, Peter and Jesus had some unfinished business to discuss. Peter had denied Jesus publicly, and Jesus knew that Peter must become stronger if he was going to be the leader that He needed Him to be. So, Jesus pulls Peter aside, and they have a talk. Three times, Jesus asks Peter if he loves Him. All three times, Peter confirms that he does. Jesus may have asked Peter this question three times to equal the amount of times that he denied Jesus.

Each time Peter answered that he loved Jesus, Jesus told him, "Feed my lambs," Take care of my sheep," and "Feed my sheep." Jesus was not asking him to take care of His livestock, but rather to step up into the role of leader of the church. In Matthew 16:18, Jesus said to Peter, "And I tell you that you are Peter, and on this rock I will build my church, and the gates of Hades will not overcome it." Peter had a calling, and yet when he felt the pressure, he lied and said that he didn't know Jesus. This had to change before Peter could help save the world.

Everyone has a mission. God has given every believer the calling to be the light of the world (Matthew 5:14) and to be an ambassador of Jesus (2 Corinthians 5:20). This calling is important to the kingdom of God, and yet, we must all step up to this calling in order to live our lives worthy of it (Ephesians 4:1). There is nothing more important in life than this. So, do you love Jesus?

Think about your gifts and talents and how God may be calling you to use them to be light and His ambassador.

Spend some time praying and reflecting over the calling you have received. You may not understand it yet, but thank God for it anyway and ask Him to help you prepare.